Marianne the Librarian

By: Julia A. Royston

Illustrated by: Derrick J. Thomas

BK Royston Publishing, Inc.

P. O. Box 4321

Jeffersonville, IN 47130

502-802-5385

www.bkroystonpublishing.com

Layout: BK Royston Publishing LLC

Illustrations by: Derrick J. Thomas

Cover Design by: Derrick J. Thomas

ISBN-13: 978-1-946111-86-9

Printed in the United States of America

Dedication

Julia Royston celebrates 30 years of librarianship in 2014. To celebrate this feat, she is dedicating this book, song and coloring book to all of the librarians in the world who have helped children and adults across the globe locate information, select a book or change their world through the power of libraries.

ACKNOWLEDGEMENTS

I thank my Lord and Savior Jesus Christ for giving me the creativity and ability to write, publish and motivate. I thank you that you have entrusted this gift to me. Lord, let your Spirit move even through this book to the people who will read it.

To my husband, Brian K. Royston, the love of my life for loving and cheering me on so much that I can be and do all that God has placed in me. I love you...

To my Mom, who is a great support and to my Dad who is in heaven but, I know is proud of me and always encouraged me to go for it. Thanks to all of my family for their love and support.

A special thank you to Rev. and Mrs. Claude R. Royston for their love and support. Papa thank you for using your fine tooth comb to edit more books than we could have ever imaged.

I acknowledge all of my supervisors, library directors and fellow librarians around the world. Know that you are not an information gatekeeper but an information distribution outlet. Information is Power!

Love, Julia A. Royston

Welcome to the Library
There's nothing you
can't know
Welcome to the Library
Walk on in, Let's Go

Books so high
It reaches to the
sky
Helpful People
abide
They all say Hi!

Computers there

Printers over there

Reference Books

Upstairs

Children's Books

Downstairs

Meet Marianne the
Librarian

Has wonderful books
to read

Marianne the
Librarian

Adventures wait and
see

Over land

Over Sea

In the Air

Come along with me

There's fun and
rhyme

Created in your
mind

There's plenty to
learn or play

Just open a book
today!

Marianne the
Librarian

Helps me to read

Marianne the
Librarian

Knows just what I
need!

Oceans wide

Mountains High

Forest trees

Animals that

please

Birds in the Sky

The Sun always
shine

Nature calls me,
hey

Open a book
today!

Marianne the
Librarian

New books she's
well aware

Marianne the
Librarian

This time it makes
me scared!

Heroes in the Air
Dragons beware
Move away from there
Oops there goes a
Bear!

I lost my way

Help me out today

The good guys saved
the day

And the bad guy is
sent away!

So visit your town library

The time is so much fun

Visit your town library

Come back, you'll read a ton!

ACTIVITY

1. Visit your local public or school library

2. Ask for help from the librarian to find your way around.

3. Find and record 3 books titles and call numbers from each section of the library

4. When you are finished, have your librarian sign the certificate at the end of the book.

5. Send a copy of the certificate to: P. O. Box 4321, Jeffersonville, IN 47131

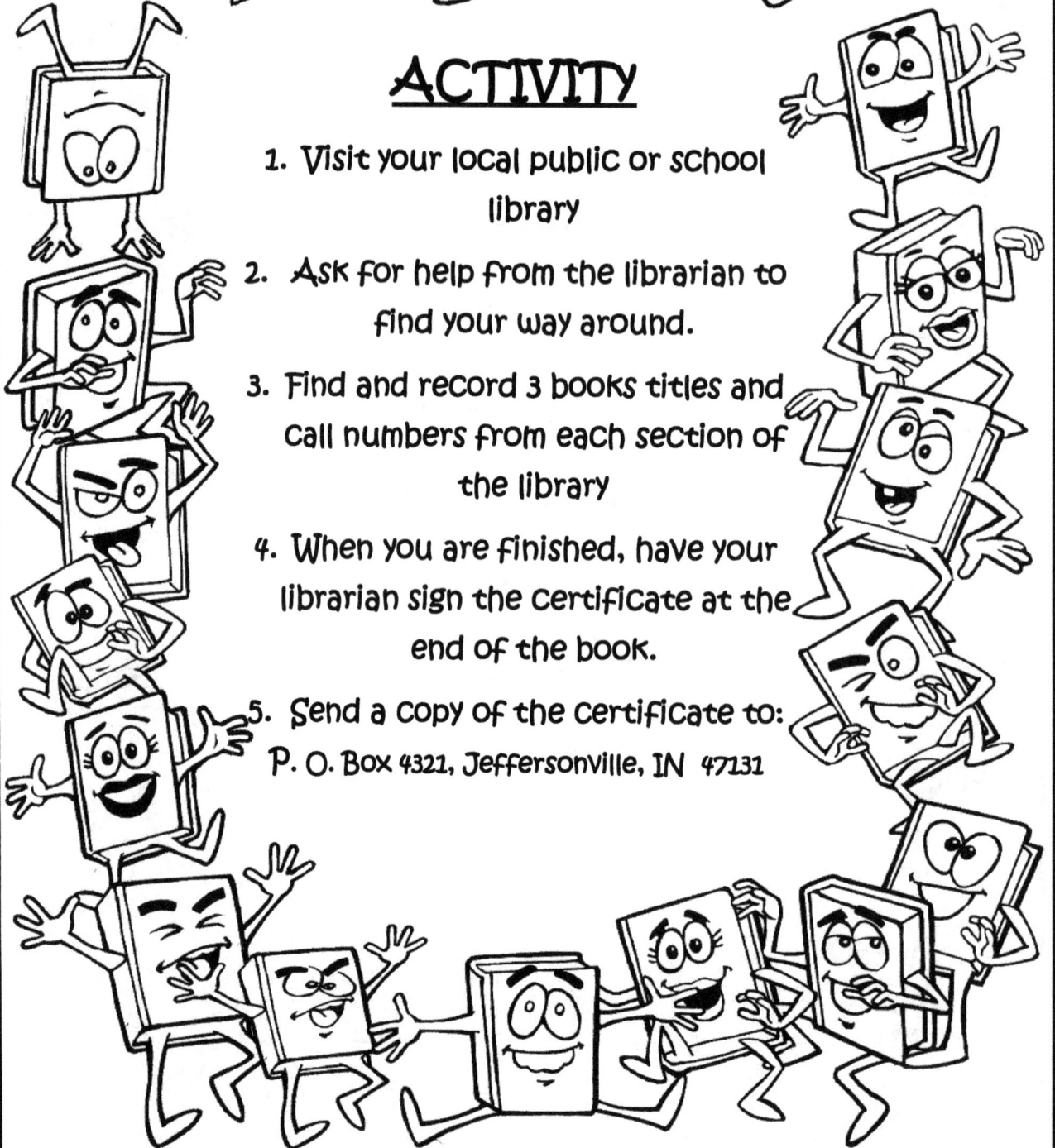

000's Generalities

(Computers, Libraries, Newspapers)

Title

_____

Call Number

_____

Title

_____

Call Number

_____

Title

_____

Call Number

_____

100's Philosophy

(Feelings, Supernatural, Animal Rights)

Title

_____

Call Number

_____

Title

_____

Call Number

_____

Title

_____

Call Number

_____

200's Religion

(Bible Stories, World Religions)

Title

_____

Call Number

_____

Title

_____

Call Number

_____

Title

_____

Call Number

_____

300's Social Sciences

(Almanacs, Government, Money, School, Holidays)

Title

_____

Call Number

_____

Title

_____

Call Number

_____

Title

_____

Call Number

_____

400's Languages

(Sign Language, Dictionaries, Grammar)

Title

_____

Call Number

_____

Title

_____

Call Number

_____

Title

_____

Call Number

_____

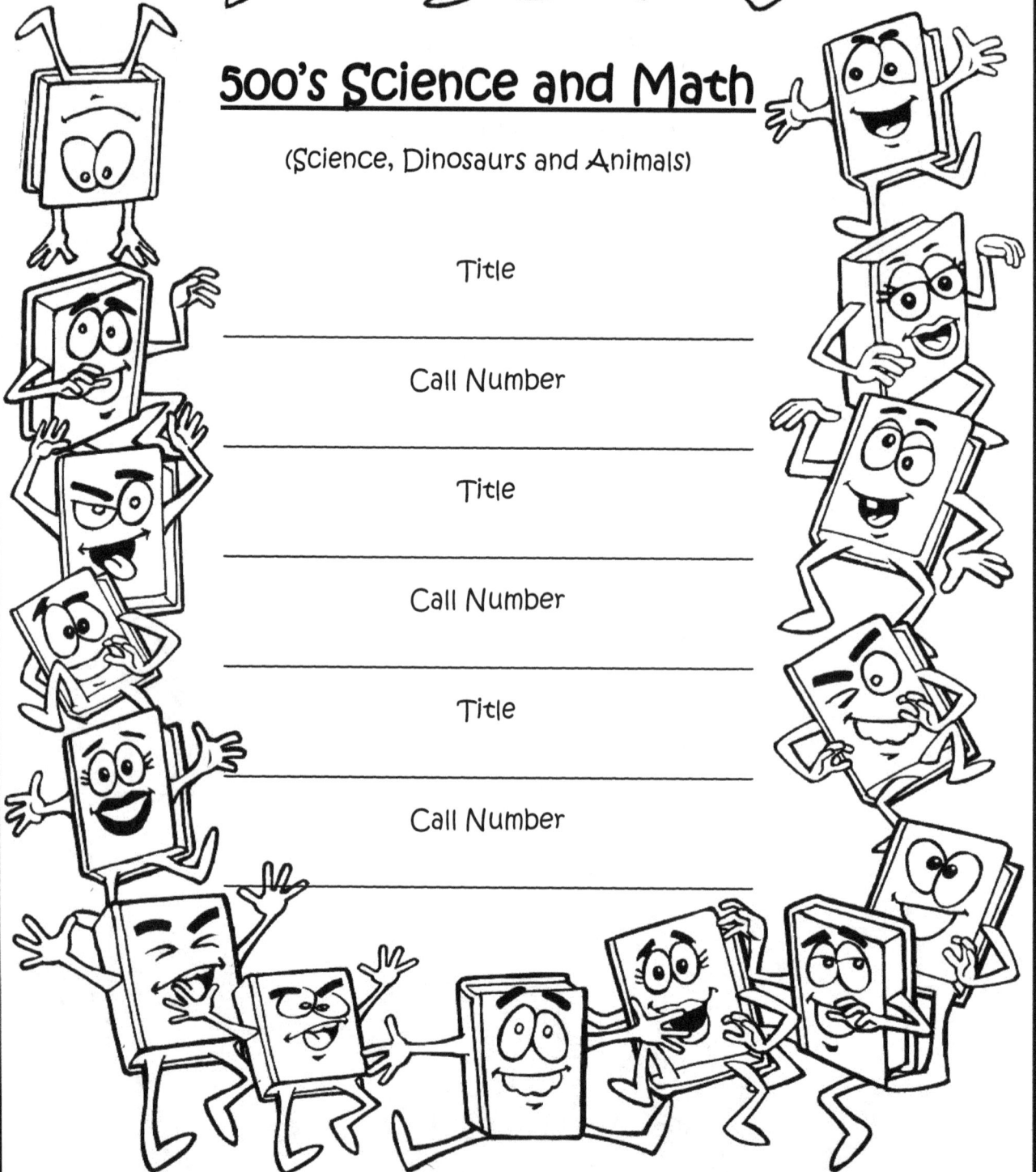

500's Science and Math

(Science, Dinosaurs and Animals)

Title

_____

Call Number

_____

Title

_____

Call Number

_____

Title

_____

Call Number

_____

600's People using Science and Technology

(Inventions, Cook Books and Secret Codes)

Title

_____

Call Number

_____

Title

_____

Call Number

_____

Title

_____

Call Number

_____

700's Arts and Recreation

(Art, Music and Sports)

Title

_____

Call Number

_____

Title

_____

Call Number

_____

Title

_____

Call Number

_____

800's Literature

(Poetry, Jokes and Riddles)

Title

_____

Call Number

_____

Title

_____

Call Number

_____

Title

_____

Call Number

_____

900's Geography and History

(Explorers, Flags and World Countries)

Title

_____

Call Number

_____

Title

_____

Call Number

_____

Title

_____

Call Number

_____

Certificate of Completion

This Certifies that

_____

Has completed the BK Royston Publishing Library Activities

_____

Librarian

_____

Library

www.ingramcontent.com/pod-product-compliance
Lightning Source LLC
Chambersburg PA
CBHW080802300326

41914CB00055B/1023